fast
fun&
easy

FABRIC FICKLESTICKS
Art Sticks to Bend, Wrap, Weave & Wear

Diana Taylor

C&T PUBLISHING

Publisher: Amy Marson

Creative Director: Gailen Runge

Editor: Stacy Chamness

Technical Editors: Nanette S. Zeller and Rebekah Genz

Copyeditor/Proofreader: Wordfirm Inc.

Cover Designer: Christina Jarumay

Book Designer: Kristy K. Zacharias

Junior Designer: Kiera Lofgreen

Production Coordinator: Zinnia Heinzmann

Illustrator: Tim Manibusan

Photography: Luke Mulks and Diane Pedersen of C&T Publishing unless otherwise noted.

Published by C&T Publishing, Inc., P.O. Box 1456, Lafayette, CA 94549

Library of Congress Cataloging-in-Publication Data

Taylor, Diana.

  Fast, fun & easy fabric ficklesticks : art sticks to bend, wrap, weave & wear / Diana Taylor.

    p. cm.

  Summary: "Instructions for making wire-filled fabric sticks that can be used to create art sculptures, jewelry, and more. Also includes a gallery of ideas to get your creative juices flowing."–Provided by publisher.

  ISBN 978-1-57120-504-9 (paper trade)

  1. Textile crafts. I. Title.

  TT699.T387 2008

  746–dc22

                            2007047136

Printed in China

10 9 8 7 6 5 4 3 2 1

Dedications

Of course, my book is dedicated to all my family and friends without whose patience and financial support I could never have spent my life stitching.

First of all, it's dedicated to my mom, a singing needleartist who taught me to sew, knit, and embroider, and to my dad, a make-and-fix-anything inventor who showed me you can do anything yourself.

To John, who took me to Burning Man the first time and who fully appreciates the creative way my brain works.

To my dear neighbor Wayne, who always liked my weird salads and other projects, and reminded me to water the yard and to clean up the house once in a while.

To Cecilia (the owner of Sew Images), who turned me on to the tube-turning tools.

Especially to my daughter Cecily, who invested the money to keep me out of the regular workforce long enough to invent ficklesticks; to my daughter Natalie, who lives with me in the chaos that is my "art"; and to my sons Abe and Nick, who have always provided the muscle for hauling my stuff around and selling my wares. And to my ex-husband, who set me up with my first craft enterprise back in 1979.

To hosts of good friends, too, who had the good sense not to offer back-handed compliments about my work, such as, "That sure is different." or "Why, I don't think I've ever thought of putting those two colors together."

Oh, and lastly, to my grandchildren whose appreciation of my creations keeps me going—particularly Maddie, who actually likes to make those darn sticks with me.

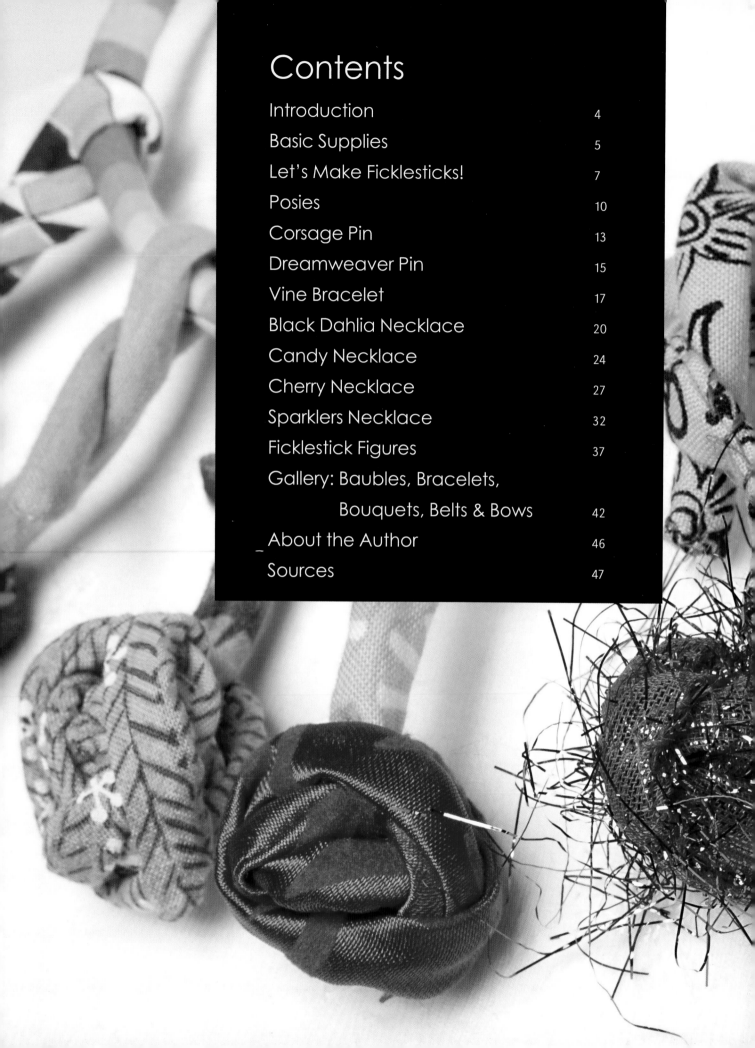

Contents

introduction

I've been making my fabric Ficklesticks of one kind or another since 2004. As difficult as it may be for you to imagine, the whole Ficklesticks thing began one sunny fall day with a spiral angel wing I was trying to fabricate for a rather weird paisley-shaped angel doll I had just created. I had folded and stitched bias tape into a narrow tube and inserted a single piece of wire, and was bending it into the spiral when bells and whistles started going off in my head! My brain was racing forward, thinking about using more exciting fabrics or even patchwork, making heavier sticks, using longer pieces of wire, weaving and building glorious things of all kinds with these fabric and wire sticks.

So, for a couple of years, I created "art" with large bendable fabric sticks: wall hangings, giant bouquets, free-standing structures, trees, baskets, stick figures, stems for giant stuffed fruit, and spindly legs for stuffed animals. I never looked back to that skinny little angel wing that started it all until the spring of 2007, when I suddenly had the urge to make sticks that were about the size of spaghetti, to see if they would lend themselves to jewelry making. I had convinced myself that I couldn't turn these tiny sticks as small as noodles right side out, but I could! Suddenly I was a jewelry designer! In the flash of an eye, I turned my attention from making huge Ficklestick structures fastened to the wall, to delicate Ficklestick corsages fastened to bosoms—just like the one featured on page 13.

Throughout 2007, I created dozens of different body adornments (some that only I have the courage to wear, admittedly), including bangles, cuffs, headbands, pendants, chokers, chains, belts, buckles, handbags, earrings, and tiny stick figures, incorporating motifs like lollipops, vines, cherries, bubblegum, flowers, and yes, even spirals.

Along the way, I definitely figured out how to make those Ficklesticks faster, more fun, and even easier. I figure I have made about 10,000 sticks by now. I hope you enjoy making these Ficklesticks projects and wearing your art jewelry as much as I do!

basic supplies

Let's make some ficklesticks!

Fabric: You will be working with 1″-wide strips of woven cottons, metallics, silks, and brocades. These can be bright, stylized patterns and solids, or more muted fabrics—your choice.

fast!

Make sure the fabrics you choose are not too thick and that there is **no** drag or nap, or else you won't be able to turn the sticks right side out. They should turn very easily.

Scissors and rotary cutters: Some fabric can be torn successfully, but scissors and rotary cutters avoid the "pulls."

Floral wire: 18″ white cloth-wrapped florist wire (36″ if you can find it). It is actually more like 'thread wrapped' and can be found at a craft store such as Jo-Ann, florist supply houses, or my website (see Sources, page 47).

Wire cutters: Any regular wire snips.

Needle-nose pliers: You will need these for coiling sticks and sometimes to help turn the sticks. These are available in practically all craft and hardware stores. Get the finest, pointiest tip you can find.

White electrical tape: The stuff electricians use. It comes in about ten colors and is available at hardware stores. White duct tape works fine, too.

Tube Turner: I use the straw and stick variety, which is also available at Jo-Ann in a 3-pack of different sizes. We will be using the smallest one (⅜″).

Ruler: This is for cutting the ficklesticks fabric pieces to specified lengths, which some of these projects call for, and for measuring and cutting wire. I always keep one of my quilting rulers stretched out on my cutting table for ease in cutting up the strips to size. I also use my handy ruler on the bottom front of my Bernina, to cut as I go.

Thread: Any all-purpose thread will do. I always use off-white for the ficklestick stitching. You will probably want an assortment of flower colors, plus green, brown, and black, too, for some hand sewing required down the road.

Needles: I always use size 14 on my sewing machine, and crewel needles for my hand sewing (bigger thread hole!).

Black elastic: I use the 3″ width down to ⅛″ black elastic cord. See individual project recommendations for specific width and yardage requirements.

Beaded chain and couplings: This comes from the hardware store and is typically used for pull chain light fixtures. Though inexpensive, it looks like silver. There are a couple of sizes; I like using the #10. The couplings are also sized to match.

Safety pins & extra strong magnets: Safety pins (I use quilters safety pins) and pin backs to hold the jewelry on can be found just about anywhere. I also use *extra-strong* magnets to attach jewelry to clothing. These magnets can be found online, at the Container Store, hardware or office supply stores, or on my website (see Sources, page 47). The typical, refrigerator-type magnets that craft stores carry are just too wimpy; look for *extra-strong* magnets.

let's make
ficklesticks!

We will start with easy, one-fabric, 6″ ficklesticks. Later, you will create longer, multi-fabric ficklesticks and versions using specific fabrics or pieced in particular ways to resemble lollipops, cherries, daisies, gumballs, and dolls' legs.

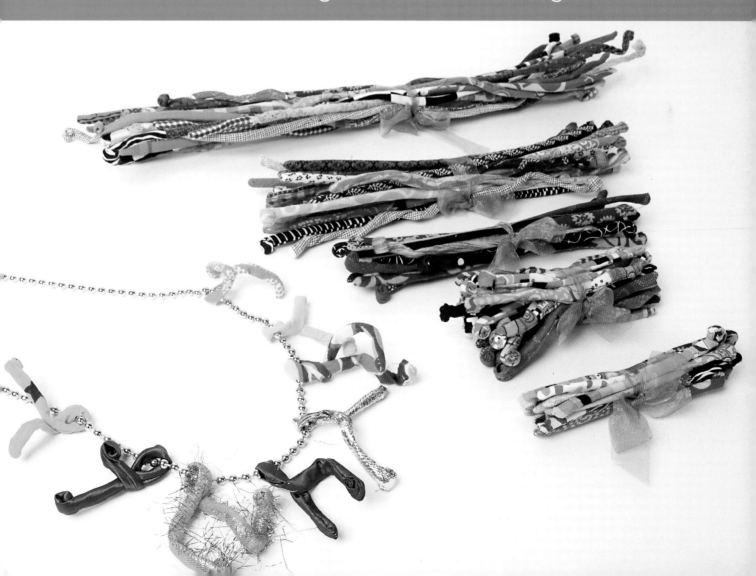

What You'll Need

- ☐ 8 fabric strips, at least 1″ × 6½″, in contrasting but coordinating fabrics
- ☐ 16 pieces of 6″-long florist wire
- ☐ Tube turner
- ☐ Electrical tape
- ☐ Needle-nose pliers

How-To

1. Gather the fabric strips and fold each lengthwise right sides together just before stitching.

2. Stitch each strip lengthwise with a ⅜″ seam, measured from the folded edge (not from the cut edge, as the strips may vary considerably in width). Stitch until you are ¼″ from the bottom edge, then make a right angle turn, continue stitching toward the folded edge. Backstitch to secure.

3. Trim each of the fabric tubes along the raw edge to a scant ¼″ seam and turn them right side out with the tube turner.

easy!

To use a tube turner, slide the straw into the fabric tube until you reach the bottom, and then push the stick back through the straw until you have turned the ficklestick right side out. It may or may not go smoothly, even if your seams are consistently ⅜″. The turning action may more closely resemble pulling the fabric down over the stick, while the stick is pushing against the sewn end and the straw remains stationary. Be careful not to poke the metal stick through the stitched end of the fabric!

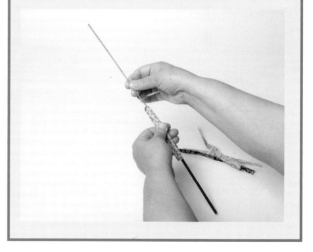

4. Cut 16 pieces of florist wire, 6″ long for each stick. Holding 2 bits of wire side by side, tape the top and bottom ends together with a small square of

EVER-CHANGEABLE FICKLESTICKS

were named for their ability to morph from one creation to another. Using the same ficklesticks again and again, you can have a candy necklace one day, 16 silent bangles the next, and a basket after that.

electrical tape at each end. This accomplishes 3 things: it keeps the wires fastened together, makes insertion smoother, and helps prevent the wires from coming back through the fabric.

easy!

If you can't find 36″ florist wire, stagger and tape 12″ or 18″ wire together.

5. Insert a pair of taped-together wires into each tube.

6. Finish the ficklesticks by trimming any excess fabric at the open end, making sure you have just enough to turn under the raw edge. Turn under the raw edge, like a flap. Now, grip this end of the stick, (flap and all) with your needle-nose pliers and make

a tiny twist, closing the end securely while neatly concealing the flap in the twist. Leave the other (stitched) end of the stick straight. Make 7 more, and you will have a nice little bundle of sticks to play with.

That's it! You have made your first ficklesticks, and you already have enough to make either the Corsage (page 13) or the Dreamweaver Pin (page 16).

fun!

Use these steps to create ficklesticks of any length. Simply increase the length of both your fabric strips and your florist wire to make 12″ or 18″ ficklesticks.

posies

Choose two contrasting fabrics to create each posy. Make sure that the fabric you want at the center of the flower is placed at the open end of the tube.

What You'll Need

- ☐ 16 fabric strips 1″ × 3½″ in contrasting colors
- ☐ 16 pieces of 6″-long floral wire
- ☐ Tube turner
- ☐ Electrical tape
- ☐ Needle-nose pliers

How-To

fast!

Cut up a whole bunch of different colored and patterned fabrics, then stitch them together in as many different combinations as you can. Surprise yourself!

1. Stitch 2 of the fabric strips together, end to end, with a ¼″ seam allowance to create a strip about 1″ × 6½″.

2. Fold each strip lengthwise and stitch with a ⅜″ seam, measured from the folded edge (not from the cut edge). Stitch until you are ¼″ from the bottom edge. Make a right angle turn, and continue stitching toward the folded edge. Backstitch to secure. Trim the raw edge to a very scant ¼″ seam allowance for ease in turning.

easy!

If the tube turner gets stuck at the joining seam, your needle-nose pliers will come in handy to drag the fabric over itself at the seam. If you have the tube turned far enough, you can take out the straw and stick, grab the exposed tip with the pliers, and yank the fabric with your other hand to get it turned over the seam. You'll get a feel for it after a while.

3. After the tube is turned, tape the ends of 2 florist wires together with a small square of electrical tape. Insert the taped wires into the tube.

4. Finish the ficklestick by folding over the raw edges like a flap. Now, grip this end of the stick (flap and all) with your needle-nose pliers and make a tiny twist, closing the end securely while neatly concealing the flap in the twist. **Be sure to leave a little "play" in the fabric so that when you roll up the posy, the wire doesn't try to force its way through the other end, and you don't create too much strain on the horizontal seam.**

5. Roll the entire ficklestick into a snug spiral, starting with the twisted end as the center. It helps to hold onto the twisted end with the needle-nose pliers as you make a tiny "jelly roll" of the stick.

fun!

As each posy gets rolled up, I enjoy seeing how the fabrics seem to bloom right before my eyes. You never know exactly where the colors will land and how the stripes and plaids will play out. One side of the flower is often very different from the other. I find it all fascinating. I usually make a couple dozen at a time.

Now you are
ready to make anything
in this book—
almost!

corsage pin

Curly chrysanthemums? Fireworks? Squids? Whatever they look like to you, they look great as a corsage! I like to mix in one or two sparkly or shiny fabrics with my cottons for extra flash.

What You'll Need

Refer to pages 8–9 for instructions on making single-fabric ficklesticks.

☐ 8 (or more!) finished 6˝ single-fabric ficklesticks

☐ Large quilters safety pin, or other pin back

☐ Needle and coordinating thread (optional)

☐ Extra-strong magnet (optional)

How-To

1. Twist a ficklestick into a loop big enough to hold the other ficklesticks.

2. Insert and twist the remaining ficklesticks through this opening. Manipulate them however you like, tightly bending and twisting them every which way until your construction doesn't have any wobbly parts and you like the way the corsage looks.

3. Weave in a large quilters safety pin as you go, or hand-stitch one on later. You may prefer to pin it on like a real corsage, with a pearly-headed hatpin.

fun!

Add some silver or gold fabrics to coordinate your corsage with your other jewelry.

fast!

I have also used extra-strong magnets to hold the pins on, having been inspired by bank teller's metal badges. This is especially good for attaching one of these pins to leather or suede. Be careful if you are wearing a coat over the pin, as you may knock it off by snagging a petal.

dreamweaver pin

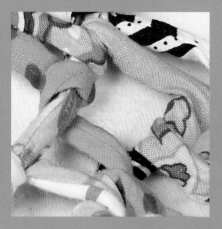

. . . Or a Secret Quilt Club Badge? This is woven and kind of dreamy, and for some reason it has always reminded me of a tiny, sixteen-block quiltlet!

What You'll Need

Refer to pages 8–9 for instructions on making single-fabric ficklesticks.

☐ 8 finished 6˝ single-fabric ficklesticks

☐ Quilters safety pin

☐ Needle and coordinating thread

How-To

1. Take 4 ficklesticks and lay them out vertically parallel to each other. Weave 1 ficklestick in horizontally, like you used to with those old potholder looms (you know, over one, under one), until you get to the other side. This will be a little cantankerous. Twist-wrap the woven ficklestick to the top and bottom horizontal sticks for security. The rest will be easy now.

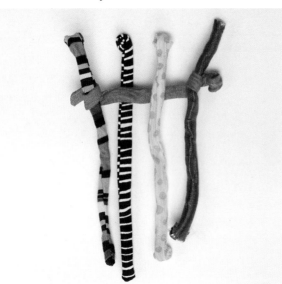

2. Weave the remaining 3 ficklesticks in the same fashion, as loosely or tightly as you like, alternating the "over one, under one" pattern with each stick.

3. Twist-wrap any untwisted sticks on the outer edges of the weaving so that all ends are secure.

fun!

If some ends are markedly longer than others, don't worry. They can be curled and twirled to great effect when you are finished weaving and twist-wrapping your pin.

4. Weave in a quilters safety pin as you go, or sew one on later.

vine bracelet

The posies on the vine bracelet should all be different but nicely coordinating—just as you would find in a well thought out garden.

What You'll Need

Refer to pages 8–9 for instructions on making single-fabric ficklesticks and posies.

☐ 1 finished 18˝ single-fabric ficklestick, for vine

☐ 3 or more finished posies

☐ Marking pencil, or pen

☐ Needle and coordinating thread

How-To

1. Twist each end of the 18˝ ficklesticks into a tight loop. This is the "vine" part of course. The vine will probably wrap around your wrist twice or more.

2. Wrap the bracelet around your wrist and make little marks where you want the posies to go. This way, you can position all the flowers on the topside of the bracelet as it fits you best.

3. Stitch the posies on by hand with thread that coordinates with the vine colors.

easy!

I hold the posy onto the vine and, from the back, stitch up one side of the vine in about three stitches and come back down the other in the same way. I tuck the straight end of the posy between the posy and the vine while I am doing the stitching, so that it is neatly trapped there.

fast!

If you like a fastened bracelet, you can bend the two ends over each other to hold the vine closed, as shown. Or, you can just loosely wrap or zigzag the vine around your wrist.

PILE ON THESE BANGLE BRACELETS.

No one will ever hear you coming!

Variations

A. **Primrose Path Cuff** While this bracelet looks sort of biker chic and a little goth, it still reminds me of a wrist supporter. Cut a piece of $1\frac{1}{2}''$ to $3''$-wide black elastic to fit around your wrist with about an inch overlap. (I always stitch the band closed by hand after I have sewn on the posies.) Attaching 4 posies is about right.

B. **Silent Bangle Bracelets** These are basically the vines without posies. Use 3–5 nicely contrasting fabrics in different lengths, from a couple of inches long to $8''$ or more. I usually stitch together the fabrics to create a giant rope and then cut that into $18\frac{1}{2}''$ lengths before stitching up the tubes. Fill the tubes as usual with 2 lengths of florist wire, taped together on both ends to make $18''$ ficklesticks. Twist both ends of the ficklesticks into tight loops, just as you did for the vines. You will probably want to wear 2 or 3 or more at a time; they are so light and fun to wear. And, they make no noise! For fun, attach solid-color posies, like giant polka dots, or join several together to wear as a choker or belt.

A

B

black dahlia
necklace

I like the weirdness of thin black elastic, so that is what I use. It stretches and it hangs well, plus you can buy it just about anywhere. Experiment with ribbon, silk cord, or strips of tulle!

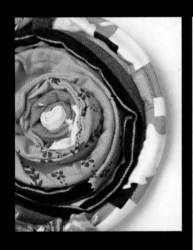

What You'll Need

Refer to pages 11–12 for instructions on making multi-fabric ficklesticks and posies.

- ☐ 60″-long piece of ⅛″ black elastic
- ☐ 18–20 finished 6″ two-fabric ficklesticks
- ☐ Needle-nose pliers (optional)

do *the twist,* and then the Charleston.

How-To

Wrap the ficklesticks into posies directly onto the elastic about 2″–2½″ apart and as tightly as you can, so they won't slip and slide later. The needle-nose pliers may be helpful here. Leave enough elastic open at the back of the necklace to tie into a nice little bow, and then wear it front or back, whichever way you like it.

fun!

Wrap finished necklace around your neck once for a flapper look, 2 or 3 times around your neck for a floating flowers look, or maybe 8 times around your wrist.

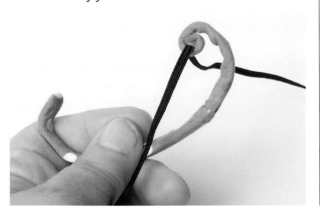

Variations

A. **Silver Dahlia Necklace** This one's a little shorter, a bit sparklier, and takes fewer posies. Cut a 40˝ piece (or your desired length) of beaded chain. Attach 8 or 9 posies by wrapping them around the chain, and close the necklace with a beaded chain coupling.

B. **Spyro-Gyra Pendant** Make a 36˝ multi-fabric ficklestick filled with 2 taped-together pieces of 36˝ wire (stagger and tape 18˝ wire together to achieve the length if you can't find 36˝ wire). Use at least 5 different fabrics with great contrast and intriguing patterns. Wrap into a giant posy, but leave 2˝ at the end to make a loop to hang from the chain and then attach that loop to the spiral with a twist. Hang the posy from about 50˝ or less of beaded chain...or something else.

C. **Spyro-Gyra Pendant, Too** Dangle a few 6˝ ficklesticks from the outside edge of the spiral for a little *je ne sais quoi.*

D. **Spinning Plate Trick Necklace** You will need 6 multi-fabric ficklesticks 18˝ long of at least 2 different fabrics each, and an additional ficklestick about 6˝ long to use as an extender (optional). Choose an 18˝ ficklestick for the neckband and wrap the other 5 onto it in the same way as the dahlia necklaces above, more or less equally spacing the plates. If you want to wear the necklace as a choker, you won't need the 6˝ extender.

E. **Escargots-A-Go-Go Choker** This is best as a choker, so you will need an 18˝ ficklestick and about 6 posies in 2 colors. Go ahead and make the posies as in the vine bracelet (page 20), then attach the posies by wrapping each "tail" tightly around the neckband. Loosen up the posy so it stands away from the band. This works on beaded chain, too.

UNCOORDINATED?
No worries, anyone can spin these plates.

A

B

C

D

E

candy necklace

These remind me of those elastic necklaces with the candy disk beads, even though this is actually a spiral with no elastic. Go figure. Use as much color and pattern as you like!

What You'll Need

Refer to pages 8–12 for instructions on making ficklesticks.

☐ 16 finished 18″ ficklesticks

How-To

1. Twist both ends of each 18″ stick into the little vine bracelet twists (page 20), and then wrap each of the sticks around your finger to make a corkscrew. Be careful you don't create some Chinese handcuffs in the process!

2. Join each of these to the next by bending the ends over each other and hiding them as best you can inside the corkscrews.

fun!

Make this as long or short as you like, even a choker. If you stretch it out, the beauty is you can always squish it back tight. You can also hang things from it, even a nice ficklesticks cross.

For the best
EYE CANDY,
be sure to use lots of
YUMMY
FABRICS!

Variations

A. **Skinny Candy Necklace** Make your corkscrews by wrapping the sticks around size 11 knitting needles.

B. **Eyeglasses Holder** You'll never look like a doddering old granny if your readers hang from a holder like this one.

C. **Candy Bracelets** Use 4 of the 18˝ ficklesticks for the big bracelet, and 2 of the 18˝ ficklesticks for the skinny one.

D. **Hatband** Roll a candy necklace onto your favorite straw hat to create a nifty hatband, or make a poinsettia band as on this green hat using the Daisy Chain variation instructions on page 32.

E. **Napkin Ring** Perfect for your next quilters luncheon. Give a set to all your favorite fabric fiends. If they'd rather wear them as bracelets or link them all together for a necklace, that's fine too!

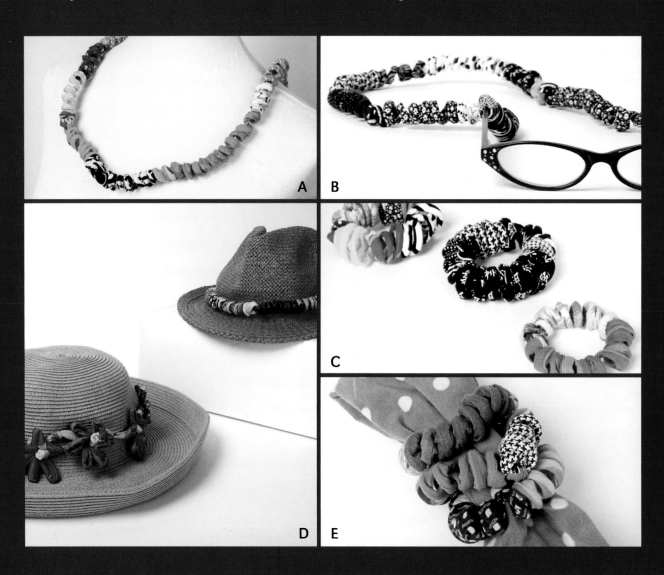

A
B
C
D
E

cherry
necklace

Curvy cherries always make a charming red and green motif. I'll show you several variations on the theme.

What You'll Need

Refer to pages 8–12 for instructions on making ficklesticks.

☐ 1 finished 18″ ficklestick, for neck cord (see Step 1, below)

☐ 5 (or more) strips 1″ × 14½″ of reds and pinks in all kinds of patterns and fabrics, for cherries

☐ 5 (or more) strips 1″ × 5″ of interesting green prints and solids, for stems

☐ 10 (or more) pieces of 18″ long florist wire

☐ Tube turner

☐ Electrical tape

☐ Needle-nose pliers

How-To

1. When making the 18″ ficklestick for your neck cord, bear in mind that the green stems of the cherries will be hanging from the center of this stick. So, make at least the center part of the neck cord in a color other than green.

easy!

Make a 6″ ficklestick extender if the neck cord is too tight.

2. To make cherry-style ficklesticks, use a ¼″ seam allowance to stitch a cherry fabric strip to a stem fabric strip in a pleasing combination. Trim the seam to a very scant ¼″ for ease in turning. Make another 4, or more!

fun!

I like to make all the cherries different and combine various textures in one necklace, so I mix brocades, satins, and even furry, metallic eyelash fabric with the more usual paisleys, plaids, dots, and other prints, even tiny printed cherries.

3. Sew the pieced strips into the usual tubes, using a ⅜″ seam, with the cherry fabric at the open end. That way, you can always begin to ball up the "cherry" with a twist, and your "stem ends" can be left uniformly straight for bending over the neckband. Fill these cherry tubes with 2 pieces of taped-together 18″ wire, and twist closed. Leave a little "play" in the fabric as you did with the posies.

4. Ball up the cherry by wrapping it loosely like balling up yarn or string, but with lots of air between the twists. Don't worry; you can try this more than once! When you get to the green part, bend at the seam and push the green part down into the cherry ball so that it looks like the stem is indeed growing out of the cherry.

5. Loop the stem over the neck cord and twist to one side as in the photo, so the danged things don't fall off! Attach the remaining cherries in the same manner.

Variations

A. **Fruit Cup** You may want to make grapes, or blueberries, or make the cherry balls different bright colors with black and white stems, or try cherries with black and white stems. Try silver or gold. Try hanging cherries from an existing chain, a length of beaded chain, or a velvet cord. You could also use beads as spacers to keep the cherries evenly spaced.

B. **Winner's Circle** How about an all-roses necklace like the horsies wear when they win the race? Well, it's not exactly like that, but it is a whole chain of flowers made the same way as the cherries above, only each is wrapped and twisted to its neighbor, flower head to stem to flower head. I like to make the flower balls mostly red, with accents of maybe orange, gold, and purple or blue.

A

B

From
STICKS
to BEADS,
BERRIES,
and . . .
bubblegum?

C. Daisy Chain Start with 8 or 9 of the 18″ multi-fabric ficklesticks made with this fabric combination: $2\frac{1}{2}$″ yellow + $12\frac{1}{2}$″ white + 5″ green. Stitch the tube making sure the yellow is placed at the open end. Fill the tubes with 2 pieces of taped-together 18″ wire, and twist the open end closed. Start by wrapping the yellow as if you were making a posy, and then loop the white around it like daisy petals. Attach the daisies to each other as you did with **Winner's Circle** (page 31)—now it's a daisy chain.

D. Balled-Up Berries Multicolored balls are fun, too. Sometimes with the right stripes and florals they almost look like marbles!

E. Beaded Blueberry Bracelet Make 9 or more 12″ single-fabric ficklesticks in blues and blue prints. Ball these up like cherries, concealing the ends by tucking them in. Cut a piece of narrow cord-style elastic about 12″ long, to string the berries on. Using a crochet hook, thread the elastic through each of the berries. Tie the elastic in a bow, or a tiny knot that you can conceal inside of a berry. This bracelet looks great with jeans!

F. Bubblegum Bracelet All in pinks and you have a bubblegum bracelet—something all the little girls in your life would love to help you make. After you string the balls on the elastic, add a fetching pink satin bow!

G. Beads, Berries & Dangles String these gumballs, marbles, berries or beads as long or short as you fancy on elastic or cording. Or use ribbon and tie with a big bow, if you like. About 20 balls makes this one.

H. Caterpillar Necklace For this you will need about $2\frac{1}{2}$ feet of $\frac{1}{8}$″ black elastic or ribbon, about 20 fun, single-fabric ficklestick "balls" made from 12″ sticks, and the same number of 6″ sticks in 1 or 2 equally punchy fabrics. Thread the balls onto the elastic or ribbon in a nicely contrasting arrangement. Loop each 6″ stick through a contrasting ball and create 2 "legs" by bending in half inside the ball and letting the legs stick out.

C

D

E

F

G

H

sparklers
necklace

This one could possibly be way over the top for fun and pizzazz. It certainly gives you something to wear to the next art opening!

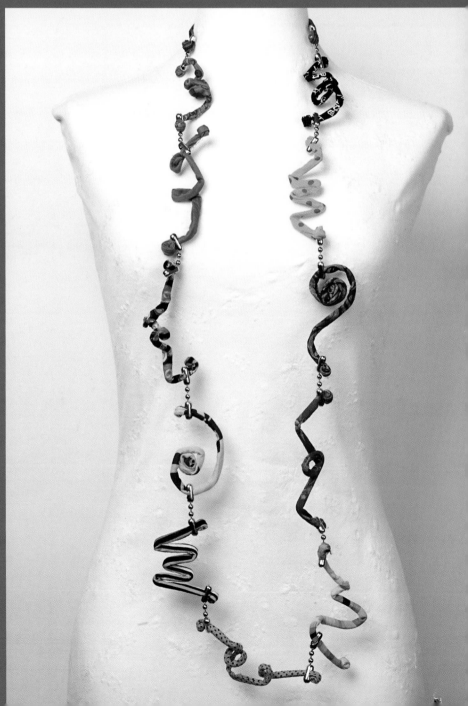

What You'll Need

Refer to pages 8–12 for instructions on making ficklesticks.

☐ 12 finished 12″ ficklesticks in outrageous patterns

☐ 24 beaded chain couplings

☐ 12 six-bead segments of beaded chain

How-To

1. Slip 2 couplings onto each ficklestick. After the couplings are on, twist the ends into tight loops so both ends of each ficklestick are now twisted. The twists keep the couplings from sliding off.

2. Between each of the sticks, you will attach a 6-bead segment of chain, inserting each end bead into the coupling of the adjoining stick.

3. Put it all together, twirling, twisting, and bending each of the ficklesticks however you like. You can slide the couplings up and down the sticks as needed for spirals and other shapes. Bend one of the ficklesticks into a smooth curve to fit around the back of your neck.

fun!

Change which ficklestick goes to the back and the way all the sticks are twisted and bent each time you wear it. Make them all corkscrews one time, all straight the next, so they really do look like sparklers!

Variations

A. Links There are several ways to make the chain links: a circle, oval, S or C shapes, or even figure eights, tiny hearts, hangers, paper clips, triangles, and squares. For fun, try combining different types and sizes of links in the same necklace.

B. All-Ficklestick Chains This one is all ficklesticks, no hardware chain, elastic, or ribbon. I like to use 9″ ficklesticks for these chain necklaces and you will need around 35 of 'em to make a chain as long as this one. Twist both ends of the sticks for uniformity, if you like.

C. Double Chain Necklace Loop sections of beaded chain (fastened to itself with a coupling) between sections of ficklestick links. It goes quickly, and the combination of shiny metal with fabric is always a nice contrast.

D. Cream Horns This can be as long or short as you like. This shorter one takes about 7 of the 12″ ficklesticks, one end twisted and one end straight, as usual. Use as many beaded chain couplings as you want "cream horns" (7 in this example). Join 6-bead segments of chain between each coupling, then add 2 lengths of 18 beads and a back closure coupling. Thread the straight end of the ficklesticks through the couplings and twirl into a cream horn shape. The twisted loop ends will hold the "mouthpieces" of the horns in place and keep the ficklestick from sliding out.

E. Shark's Teeth Assemble the chain as with the Cream Horns, but use shorter 6″ ficklesticks, curving them slightly to look like teeth. Or make wavy teeth. Or make them all red-orange like coral or shrimp.

SWAG
your neck, your beltline, your Christmas tree, or even a doorway.

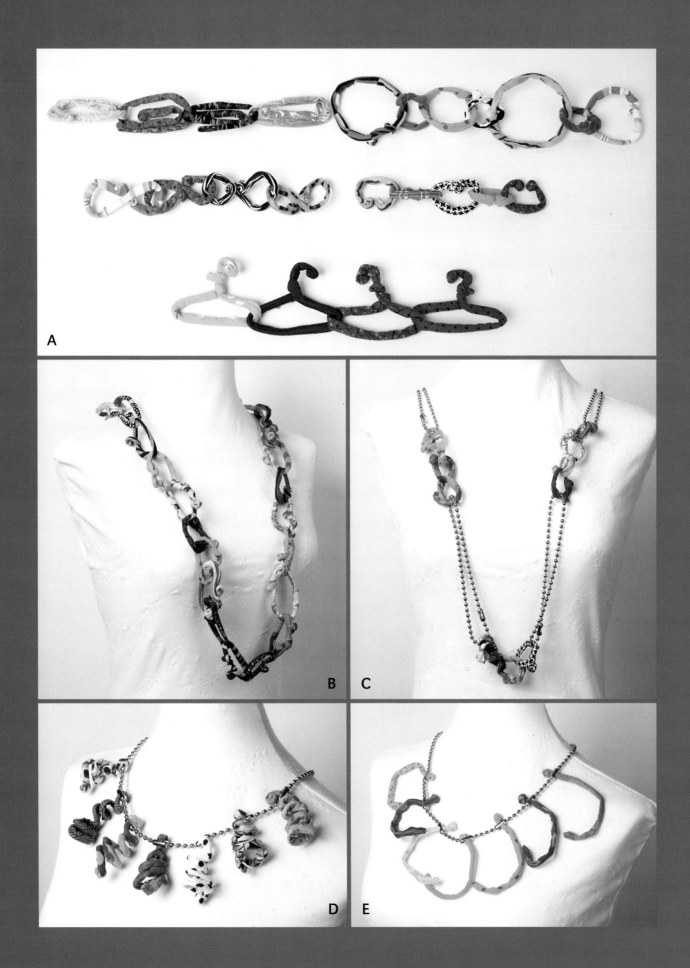

F. **All-Purpose** Try hanging other things, too—like a fake pair of ficklesticks glasses, a cross, ficklestick figures, and the like.

G. **Ladder Necklace** Make your ladder with 6 of the 6˝ ficklesticks, as usual, leaving one end straight on each stick. Use these to make 2 side supports and 4 rungs of a ladder (see page 17). Be sure to put the straight ends of the side supports at the same end so you can slide on the beaded chain couplings after the ladder is made. Attach a coupling to each straight end of the ladder side support, then twist the ends of the ladder to keep the coupling from falling off. Take two 16˝ pieces of beaded chain and attach one piece to each ladder coupling. Attach another coupling at the back of the neck to join the pieces of chain.

H. **Lollipops** Begin by stitching up 8 of the 12˝ ficklesticks, as usual, leave one end straight for threading onto the couplings. Or, if you think you would like a less flamboyant necklace, try using 9˝ or even 6˝ sticks. Coil the sticks into rather tight spirals, and then slide 2 couplings onto each stick. Position these so they are opposite each other and far enough into the spiral so that they won't slip off. Attach these together with 16-bead sections of chain, and finish the neck edge off with 24-bead sections on both ends, as well as another coupling at the back of the neck.

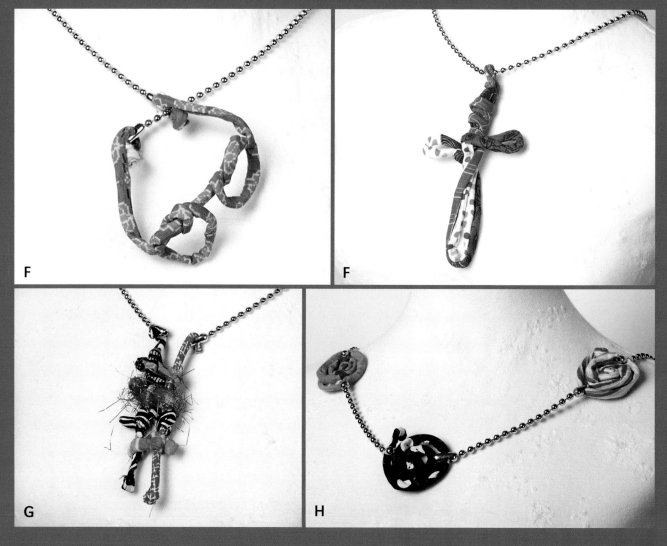

F

F

G

H

ficklestick figures

These adorable little stick figures are small enough to wear as pins, and link together like paper dolls for an outrageous necklace, tree garland, or even baby room décor! Create some of your own versions—maybe a chef, leprechaun, cowboy, soldier, ninja, or a bride and groom!

What You'll Need

Refer to pages 8–12 for instructions on making ficklesticks.

☐ *For each figure:* 3 finished 12˝ ficklesticks

☐ Scrap of skin tone or coordinating fabric, for head

☐ Small quantity of fiberfill stuffing, for head

☐ Needle and coordinating thread

How-To

For each figure you will need 3 ficklesticks. Make multi-fabric sticks in assorted colors and patterns or use one fabric per stick. Just remember 2 sticks are used for the body and legs, and 1 stick is used for the arms.

Head
Cut 2.

Head pattern

1. Trace the head and sew with a very narrow seam. Leave an opening at the neck edge to turn, to stuff, and to insert onto the body.

fast!

Because it is so small I like to trace the head on fabric, stitch it, and *then* cut it out. This makes it way easier to manipulate.

2. Choose 2 ficklesticks for the body and legs. With the straight ends up, tie the middle of the sticks into a fairly loose overhand knot (creating a butt for the stick figure). The front side is the side with the horizontal pass of the knot. The 2 twisted closed ends of the ficklesticks are the legs and the straight ends form the torso and neck.

Neck

Legs

easy!

Clipping a tunnel into the stuffing at the neck opening will make it go on more easily.

3. Pull a turned-and-stuffed head onto the neck, turning under raw edges and stitching with invisible stitches.

4. Place the arm stick at shoulder level on the figure. The right arm, as it faces you, should be about an inch shorter than the left. The left arm will do most of the wrapping and take up that extra length.

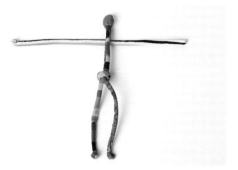

5. While holding the arms in place, wrap the right arm across the front, over the left shoulder, and around the back to the starting position.

6. Wrap the left arm across the front, over the right arm, and around to the back to the starting position.

7. Make one final wrap by taking the left arm and creating a diagonal cross on the front and under the right arm, around to the back, and finally into its starting position. Wrap tightly! You can always re-wrap if one arm ends up noticeably longer than the other.

8. Now twist remaining ends, crook the elbows, and bend the knees and feet. Your stick figure is ready for a few yoga poses.

fun!

To make a witch hat, align both hat triangles, right sides facing, and join with a very scant seam up one side to a point. Position and sew the hat brim to the bottom edge of the sewn triangles. Sew the final side seam from brim to tip in one fell swoop, sort of like you would sew a side seam and sleeve in a garment all at once. Trim the seams and turn the hat so that the seams face inside.

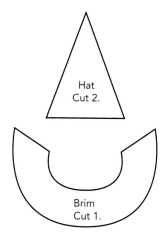

Hat pattern, and brim for witch hat.

Variations

A. **Santa** Make Santa in reds and greens and use the hat pattern without the brim (above) to sew a tiny felt cap. Add a bit of soft wool for his beard. If you like, give him a tiny bag for holding a very special gift. Try a Santa in sparkly reds or satin PJs.

B. **Ballerina** Make a tiny tutu by cutting a piece of tulle about 6″ × 9″. Fold in thirds so it measures 6″ × 3″. Hand stitch a gathering stitch along the long edge and gather it onto the ballerina's waist, then stitch closed.

C. **Witch** Make 2 sticks, sewing a 2½″ piece of orange-and-white striped fabric (for the stockings) to 1″ black pieces (for the shoes). Attach the other end of the striped stockings to 9½″ pieces of a fetching black print to make the mini skirt and bodice. Make a third stick with 2 pieces 1¾″ of pale green at each end for her hands with another 9½″ piece of the black print sandwiched between. Don't forget her sickly green head. Use the hat pattern (above) to cut and make a hat from black felt then add a brim. You may want to stitch the hat by hand. Add hair, a black kitty cat, and tiny broom!

D. **Angel** I hesitate to give a wing pattern, as there are so many kinds of wings. I rather like this felt wing with paper-punched holes.

E. **Rag Doll** Make her as you did the witch, substituting a red-and-white stripe for the socks (or some other color), a nice little paisley or polka dot for the black print, and skin tone for the sickly green! Add a tuft of loopy hair and sew on a tiny, red felt heart.

F. **Clown** Make 3 sticks using assorted polka dots or fabric of your choice. Attach liberated fringe balls to the front of his outfit like buttons, add a pointed hat or bald bozo-style head with orange fringe, and finish with a ruffled collar of tulle. Use fabric markers as clown paint!

FICKLESTICK
FIGURES
all get jobs!

A

B

C

D

E

F

baubles, bracelets, bouquets, belts & bows

You are probably already thinking of lots of things you want to make! Ficklesticks are so versatile: they can be a necklace one day, a hat band the next, and then bows on a package later. They're so fickle!

A. Wrap vine bracelets through belt loops on jeans or try making a striped grosgrain ribbon belt with 2 ficklesticks rings for closure. For a real showstopper, find some wide double-sided satin ribbon and make a ficklestick buckle and corsage pin closure. It just bends shut!

B. Take a posy, attach it to a small rubber band or hair band, and make a ring or ponytail holder.

C. Headbands use vines, posies, cherries, and plain ficklesticks to great effect. There might be a bridal party application here!

D. Accessorize your shoes!

E. Use some wide sheer ribbon or a length of tulle to make this scarf.

B

C

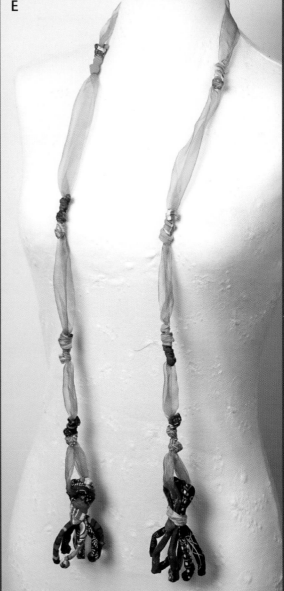

E

D

F. Decorate an existing purse, or make one out of washed wool felt lined with satin, like I did. Embellish its flap with dangly sticks and cherries. Make a moldable strap by joining sections of various ficklesticks together: vines, cherries, flowers, and plain sticks.

G. Here's the Black Dahlia on a green cord.

H. Wrap a hat with a couple of vine bracelets, join some flowers into a hatband, dangle berries like ball fringe, or even hide a logo under a bodacious medallion like I did here! Make a hat using only sticks!

I. You can find hooks and loops at a bead or craft store to make your own ficklestick earrings.

J. Your macramé wall hanging could be a lot more complicated than this. I used 16 of the 36″ sticks and a skinny piece of bamboo. I know you old timers probably have a least one macramé book where you could find some better looking knots than these!

K. 12″ sticks woven together make this little basket. Use longer ficklesticks, and lots more of them, for bigger weavings.

L. Stand up those cherries (masquerading as roses) or daisies in a tiny vase, or bundle them and pin to your jacket. They also make a great gift package trim. Be sure to make some of these space-age flowers, using the spinning plate tricks technique with 9″ or 12″ stems and regular posies or other 6″ "coins."

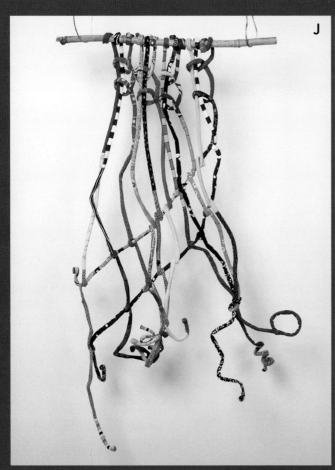

M. Decorate packages with pretty bows.

N. Spell out letters, or even words!

about the author

Diana Taylor was born in Lafayette, Indiana, the oldest of four. She attended Purdue University briefly as a "Hoosier Scholar," and managed two art-related courses before leaving to marry at the age of eighteen. She raised four children as a military wife in Spain, Holland, and in the South. By 1981, after a couple of years consigning her work and selling at crafts shows, she established "Granny's Fan," a cottage-industry manufacturer of softly-sculpted items from vintage fabrics. She took the company to market where she secured orders from Macy's, Bloomingdale's, the American Folk Art Museum, and dozens of other retailers. Diana closed the company in 1989, went on to work for Leisure Arts briefly, and then spent fifteen years as a newspaper-advertising executive in Little Rock. During this time, she also rescued a historic house, joined the Arkansas Quilters Guild, traveled in the U.S., Europe, Asia, and South America, and was a founding member of the Little Rock Wind Symphony, where she played clarinet for ten years.

After 25 years in Arkansas, she left for the San Francisco Bay Area in 2003 to be near her grown children and grandchildren who had all arrived, one by one, ahead of her. She had planned to sell real estate, frolic in the bay, and play clarinet in a band in San Francisco. Instead, in 2004 she established Stickball, an artware studio producing a full line of ficklesticks "art" being sold in museum gift shops, artisan galleries, and other boutiques across the U.S. She gave up real estate and found out the bay was too cold, but she is still playing in the band. *Fast, Fun & Easy Fabric Ficklesticks* is her first book.

sources

Extra-Strong Magnets
Diana Taylor
www.stickballstudio.com

Three by Three Seattle (Wholesale orders only)
 1518 NW 52nd Street
 Seattle, WA 98107
 (206) 784-5839
 www.threebythree.com

Sewing supplies, machines, and services
Sew Images
 1472 Piedmont Ave.
 Oakland, CA 94611
 (510) 601-8739
 www.sewimages.com

Stonemountain and Daughter
 2518 Shattuck Ave
 Berkeley, CA 94704
 (510) 845-6106
 www.stonemountainfabric.com

Turn-It-All Fabric Tube Turner
Hancock Fabrics
 1 Fashion Way
 Baldwyn, MS 38824
 (877) FABRICS (322-7427)
 www.hancockfabrics.com

White cloth-covered floral stem wire
Diana Taylor
 www.stickballstudio.com

Panacea Products Corp. (Wholesale orders only)
 2711 International St.
 Columbus, OH 43228
 (614) 850-7000

CreateForLess
 6932 SW Macadam Ave.—Suite A
 Portland, OR 97219
 www.createforless.com

Jo-Ann Fabric & Crafts
 Find your local Jo-Ann store at *www.joann.com*

White electrical tape, beaded chain, and couplings
Ace Hardware
 Find your local Ace at
 www.acehardware.com

For a list of other fine books from C&T Publishing, ask for a free catalog:
C&T Publishing, Inc.
 P.O. Box 1456
 Lafayette, CA 94549
 (800) 284-1114
 ctinfo@ctpub.com
 www.ctpub.com

C&T Publishing's professional photography services are now available to the public. Visit us at www.ctmediaservices.com.

For quilting supplies:
Cotton Patch
 1025 Brown Ave.
 Lafayette, CA 94549
 (800) 835-4418
 www.quiltusa.com

Note: *Fabrics used in the Ficklesticks shown may not be currently available, as fabric manufacturers keep most fabrics in print for only a short time.*

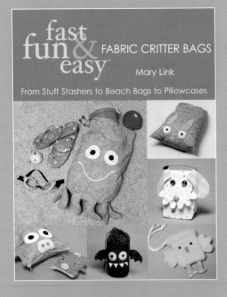
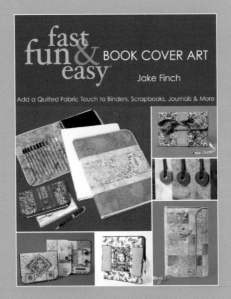

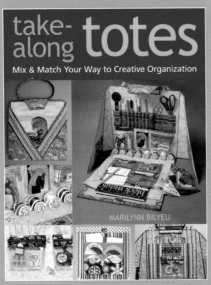